The Ultimate Pressure Cooker Book

with
Debra Murray

acknowledgements

I am so blessed to be able to create and share this cookbook. It is the culmination of so many talented and supportive people:

First, I would like to thank my incredible family. My beloved husband Martin, my bright and beautiful daughter Nevar, my incredible parents Yvette and Reggie, my devoted sister Gail as well as my darling step grand children Brennan and Patrick. Your love and encouragement is the fuel that drives everything I do. I also want to dedicate this book to the memory of Martin B. Murray III.

I would like to thank Wolfgang Puck, my incredible boss, friend and mentor. You not only taught me how to cook, but how to live, love and laugh. Thank you for allowing me to publish these cookbooks. It is a dream come true for me and I treasure the 12 years we have worked together.

Thank you to Sydney Silverman for running this remarkable company and for your commitment to service and quality. Mike Sanseverino, bless you for engineering this brilliant pressure cooker. It is literally going to change the world for the better.

Thank you to Jonathan Schwartz and Daniel Koren. These books are the outcome of your talents and hard work. Thank you for all you do.

Thank you to Marian Getz, who not only works so hard to bring all of our cooking shows to life, but teaches me many hidden cooking secrets that no one has ever published. I am so grateful for every minute we spend together.

Thank you to Chris Davis, my brilliant photographer. I cherish every second we work together. Your goodness is so inspiring.

Thank you to Tracy Ferguson, my talented food stylist as well as Cameron Fritz for your hard work.

Thank you to Tina and Tony Herrell for the use of their home to take photographs.

Thanks to everyone who reaches out to me by email, the rice cooker group or the pressure cooker group. I would also like to thank the people from my church.

Most of all I want to thank the kind HSN viewers who purchase our products and books. It is all your love and support that deserves the biggest thank you. God Bless you all.

The pressure cooker is surrounded by stories ranging from lids flying off to soup dripping from the ceiling. While older pressure cookers may have caused these episodes, today's generation of pressure cookers are modified to ensure safe and easy cooking. This appliance is designed to use steam pressure to break down the fibers of the food, allowing for faster cooking times. Tough meats become tender quickly, vegetables and grains are infused with flavors and foods retain their nutrients. Although the pressure cooker is mainly used as a timesaving device, it works for fine cooking as well.

Debra Murray has been my assistant at the Home Shopping Network for over 12 years, and I know her passion for quality appliances that can make anyone a better cook. Debra knows how to use the pressure cooker in remarkable ways. Her passion for cooking and experimental nature created this amazing collection of recipes. I have urged her to share them with as many people as possible through this book.

An extremely talented cook, Debra shares my WELL (Wolfgang's Eat, Love, Live!™) philosophy of good cooking and warm hospitality. I believe everyone should use the freshest, all-natural ingredients, locally grown, organic when possible, and raised using sustainable humane methods.

I learned long ago, beside my mother and grandmother, one should always put lots of love into cooking. This is evident in this book of Debra Murray's pressure cooker recipes.

Wolfgang Puck

table of contents

- It is very important to have a liquid such as water, stock, juice or wine in the pressure cooker in order to create steam. Thicker liquids such as barbecue or tomato sauce will not create steam. At least 1 to 2 cups of liquid are necessary to create adequate steam.

- When converting these recipes for pressure cookers other than the Wolfgang Puck pressure cooker, use your low pressure setting for recipes using the VEGGIE function. For all other recipes in this book, use your high pressure setting.

- When cooking a rice, bean or pasta dish, do not fill the pressure cooker more than halfway. When cooking soups or stocks, do not exceed the $2/3$ mark.

- If you live in higher altitudes, you may increase the cooking time slightly. I suggest adding 5% cooking time for every 1000 feet above sea level.

- All of the recipes were tested by weight so if you wish to cook a larger piece of meat, you will need to increase the cooking time. Add 10 minutes to the suggested cooking time for every additional pound of meat.

- Every piece of meat is not graded or marbled with the same amount of fat and cooking time adjustments may be necessary. If your meat is not as tender as you would like, simply add ½ cup of liquid and increase the cooking time by 10 minutes.

- Here are some guidelines for rice that work for me: On the RICE function, white rice cooks in 6 minutes, brown or wild rice cooks in 20 minutes.

- The valves and regulator need to be clean for the pressure cooker to function properly. Wash the lid and remove the regulator for cleaning. The gasket should always be hand washed and properly fitted back on the lid as it prevents the steam from escaping. If not properly installed, steam will escape under the lid and pressure will not be achieved.

- I do not recommend using the quick release method for letting the pressure out. I have timed the recipes in this book with the pressure going out on its own. Remember to never attempt to open the lid while pressure cooking is in progress.

- If you every complete a recipe and the cooking liquid is thinner than you desire, simply press the RICE function and let the liquid reduce with the lid off until the desired consistency is achieved.

Please use the chart below for your reference:

INGREDIENT	AMOUNT	FUNCTION (Minutes)	TIME SUGGESTED	LIQUID (Cups)
VEGETABLES				
Artichokes, trimmed	3 med	Veggie	14	2
Beans, Black	1 cup	Veggie	12	2
Beans, Navy	1 cup	Veggie	8	2 - 2 1/2
Beans, Pinto	1 cup	Rice	15	3
Beans, Red Kidney	1 cup	Rice	20	3 1/2
Beans, String	1 lb	Veggie	3	1
Beets	6 med	Veggie	15	2
Cabbage head, quartered	1 med	Veggie	10	2
Carrots 2" pieces	2 cups	Veggie	5	1
Corn on the cob	6 ears	Veggie	4	1 1/2
Parsnips, cubed	2 cups	Veggie	4	1 1/2
Squash , Acorn, halved	4 halves	Veggie	13	2
Squash, Butternut, 1/2" slices	8 slices	Veggie	4	1 1/2
MEATS, POULTRY, SEAFOOD				
Beef Brisket	3 lbs	Meat	90	2-3
Beef Ribs	6 whole	Meat	30	2
Chicken, boneless, skinless pieces, frozen	4 lbs	Meat	5	2
Chicken, legs	4 whole	Meat	20	2
Chicken, quartered	1 whole	Meat	20	2
Chicken, whole	3 lbs	Meat	20	3
Chuck Roast	3 lbs	Meat	75	2-3
Corned Beef	3 lbs	Meat	90	3
Baby Back Ribs	2 slabs	Meat	20	2
Lamb Shanks	2-3 lbs	Meat	30	2
Pork Chops (8-10 oz each)	3-4	Meat	12	2
Pork Loin	2 lbs	Meat	22	3
Short Ribs	3 lbs	Meat	35	2
Spare Ribs	1 slab	Meat	30	2
Stew Meat 1" pieces	3 lbs	Meat	18	4
Turkey Breast	5 lbs	Meat	45	3
Veal Shanks (8 oz each)	3	Meat	30	2
POTATOES				
Potato, Baking	4 large	Veggie	15	2
Potatoes, Red Bliss (2 oz each)	up to 20	Veggie	7	2
Potatoes, White, cubed	3 cups	Veggie	5	1 1/2

soups & stews

fresh vegetable soup

makes 6 servings

INGREDIENTS

½ cup sweet onions, diced
3 garlic cloves, sliced
¼ cup celery, diced
¼ cup carrots, peeled and sliced
¼ cup celery root, peeled and diced
¼ cup green beans, cut into ½-inch pieces
¼ cup fresh corn kernels
¼ cup Brussels sprouts, diced
1 can (14.5 ounces) petite diced tomatoes
3 cups beef stock
1 teaspoon sea salt
1 teaspoon freshly ground pepper
1 sprig fresh thyme

1. Place all ingredients into the pressure cooker; secure lid.

2. Set pressure cooker to SOUP and timer to 10 minutes.

3. When cooking is complete, remove thyme sprig and serve.

ginger carrot soup

makes 4 to 6 servings

INGREDIENTS

6 large carrots, peeled and chopped
1 medium onion, diced
2 tablespoons fresh ginger, minced
2 cups chicken stock
½ cup orange juice
1 teaspoon salt
½ teaspoon freshly ground pepper

1. Place all ingredients into the pressure cooker; secure lid.

2. Set pressure cooker to SOUP and timer to 5 minutes.

3. When cooking is complete, purée soup in a blender and serve.

15 bean soup

makes 4 to 6 servings

INGREDIENTS

1 pound 15 bean soup mix
1 large onion, diced
1 can (28 ounces) crushed tomatoes
3 celery stalks, chopped
1 ham hock
1 pound pork shoulder, diced into 1-inch cubes
2 garlic cloves, minced
1 tablespoon parsley
1 teaspoon rosemary
2 teaspoons salt
1 teaspoon black pepper
8 cups chicken stock

1. Place all ingredients into the pressure cooker; secure lid.

2. Set pressure cooker to SOUP and timer to 30 minutes.

3. When cooking is complete, remove ham hock and serve.

split pea soup

makes 6 to 8 servings

INGREDIENTS

1 package (16 ounces) split peas with seasoning packet
2 cups pork shoulder, diced
3 carrots, peeled and sliced
½ cup onions, diced
2 celery stalks, sliced
2 garlic cloves, minced
1 bay leaf
2 tablespoons fresh parsley, chopped
1 tablespoon salt
½ teaspoon freshly ground pepper
1 teaspoon vinegar
6 cups water

1. Place all ingredients into the pressure cooker; secure lid.

2. Set pressure cooker to SOUP and timer to 10 minutes.

3. When cooking is complete, remove bay leaf and serve.

tomato florentine

makes 4 to 6 servings

INGREDIENTS

2 pounds grape tomatoes
6 cups chicken stock
1 medium onion, chopped
1 carrot, peeled and sliced
3 garlic cloves, sliced
1 teaspoon salt
1 teaspoon freshly ground pepper
1 cup dry pasta
1 cup baby spinach leaves
5 basil leaves, torn

1. Place all ingredients, except basil, into the pressure cooker; secure lid.

2. Set pressure cooker to SOUP and timer to 8 minutes.

3. When cooking is complete, top with basil and serve.

Deb's Tip:
Garnish with a touch of pesto.

kabocha squash soup

makes 4 to 6 servings

INGREDIENTS

1 (2.5 pound) kabocha squash, peeled, seeded and cut into 2-inch pieces
1 small onion, chopped
2 tablespoons ginger, sliced
3 garlic cloves
1 teaspoon salt
1 teaspoon freshly ground pepper
2 cups chicken stock
¼ cup orange juice
1 tablespoon brown sugar

1. Place all ingredients into the pressure cooker; secure lid.

2. Set pressure cooker to SOUP and timer to 10 minutes.

3. When cooking is complete, purée the soup using an immersion blender until desired consistency and serve.

(Deb's Tip:
Garnish with sour cream and cranberry sauce.)

hot sour noodle soup with shrimp

makes 4 to 6 servings

INGREDIENTS

5 cups chicken stock
4 garlic cloves, sliced
1 tablespoon fresh ginger, grated
1 star anise
3 tablespoons fish sauce
1 tablespoon soy sauce
1 teaspoon brown sugar
1 Serrano chili pepper, seeds and membrane removed, thinly sliced
1 lemongrass stalk, halved
1 teaspoon lime zest
1 tablespoon lime juice
1 pound shrimp, peeled and deveined
2 cups bean sprouts
2 green onions, cut into 1-inch pieces
2 tablespoons cilantro leaves, chopped
2 tablespoons fresh mint leaves, chopped
6 ounces rice noodles, cooked

1. Place all ingredients, except rice noodles, into the pressure cooker; secure lid.

2. Set pressure cooker to SOUP and timer to 10 minutes.

3. When cooking is complete, remove the lemongrass then add the rice noodles to the pressure cooker; stir.

4. Divide the soup between bowls and serve.

martin's lobster asparagus soup

makes 4 servings

INGREDIENTS

2 cups chicken stock
1 cup white wine
1 lemon, halved
1 leek (white part only), sliced
1 celery stalk
2 lobster tails, with shells
1 teaspoon lemon pepper seasoning
1 pound fresh asparagus, cut into 1-inch pieces
4 ounces cream cheese

1. Place all ingredients, except cream cheese, into the pressure cooker; secure lid.

2. Set pressure cooker to SOUP and timer to 10 minutes.

3. When cooking is complete, remove the lobster meat from the tails and discard the shells.

4. Cut the lobster meat into 1/2-inch pieces and place them back into the pressure cooker.

5. Add the cream cheese to the pressure cooker and stir until dissolved.

6. Serve hot or cold.

shrimp bisque

makes 4 to 6 servings

INGREDIENTS

2 pounds large shrimp, with shells
2 tablespoons extra-virgin olive oil
1 teaspoon salt
1 teaspoon freshly ground pepper
1 teaspoon sweet paprika
1 cup white wine
1 carrot, peeled and chopped
1 celery stalk, chopped

1 leek (white part only), sliced
1 garlic clove, sliced
1 small potato, peeled and halved
1 tablespoon tomato paste
3 cups chicken stock
1 sprig tarragon
2 teaspoons sherry
1 cup heavy cream

1. Dry the shrimp using paper towels.

2. Preheat the oil in a sauté pan over medium-high heat.

3. Add the shrimp to the pan and cook for 3 minutes on each side.

4. Season the shrimp with salt, pepper and paprika then transfer them to the pressure cooker.

5. Add the wine to the pan; scrape up all the little bits from the bottom of the pan then transfer the pan contents to the pressure cooker.

6. Add remaining ingredients, except heavy cream, to the pressure cooker; secure lid.

7. Set pressure cooker to SOUP and timer to 6 minutes.

8. When cooking is complete, remove the tarragon sprig.

9. Using an immersion blender, purée the soup while adding the cream; purée until desired consistency before serving.

potato leek soup

makes 4 to 6 servings

INGREDIENTS

2 cups leeks (white part only), sliced
1 cup sweet onions, sliced
2 cups Yukon Gold potatoes, peeled and diced
3 cups chicken stock
½ teaspoon salt
½ teaspoon freshly ground pepper
½ cup sour cream
1 teaspoon fresh chives, chopped

1. Place all ingredients, except sour cream and chives, into the pressure cooker; secure lid.

2. Set pressure cooker to SOUP and timer to 10 minutes.

3. When cooking is complete, purée the soup using an immersion blender until desired consistency.

4. Serve topped with sour cream and chives.

Deb's Tip:
This soup is even more delicious served cold.

pizza soup

makes 4 to 6 servings

INGREDIENTS

1 can (28 ounces) petite diced tomatoes
1 medium onion, chopped
4 garlic cloves, sliced
4 cups chicken stock
1 teaspoon salt
1 teaspoon freshly ground pepper
1 teaspoon dried oregano
1 pound Italian turkey sausage, thinly sliced
3 ounces turkey pepperoni, diced
1 green bell pepper, diced
½ cup dry ditalini pasta
½ cup mozzarella cheese, shredded

1. Place all ingredients, except mozzarella cheese, into the pressure cooker; secure lid.

2. Set pressure cooker to SOUP and timer to 8 minutes.

3. When cooking is complete, divide the soup between bowls, top with cheese and serve.

(**Deb's Tip:**
Serve with a piece of garlic bread on the side.)

french onion soup

makes 4 to 6 servings

INGREDIENTS

4 large sweet onions, sliced
2 cups beef stock
1 tablespoon balsamic vinegar
¼ cup red wine
2 sprigs thyme
1 bay leaf
½ teaspoon salt
½ teaspoon freshly ground pepper
8 ounces gruyere cheese, sliced

1. Place all ingredients, except cheese, into the pressure cooker; secure lid.

2. Set pressure cooker to SOUP and timer to 20 minutes.

3. When cooking is complete, remove thyme and bay leaf.

4. Turn oven to broil.

5. Ladle soup into oven-safe bowls then top each bowl with 2 slices of cheese.

6. Place bowls under the broiler for 2 minutes or until cheese is melted.

7. Serve immediately.

lentils with italian turkey sausage

makes 4 servings

INGREDIENTS

1 pound sweet Italian turkey sausage, cut into 1-inch pieces
1 medium onion, diced
2 garlic cloves, sliced
1 large carrot, peeled and thinly sliced
1 celery stalk, thinly sliced
1 cup lentils
2 cups chicken stock
1 can (14.5 ounces) diced tomatoes with garlic and olive oil
1 bay leaf
½ teaspoon crushed red pepper flakes (optional)

1. Place all ingredients into the pressure cooker; stir then secure the lid.

2. Set pressure cooker to MEAT and timer to 20 minutes.

3. When cooking is complete, discard the bay leaf and serve.

low country boil

makes 4 to 6 servings

INGREDIENTS

5 cups water
1 cup white wine
1 medium onion, quartered
4 whole garlic cloves
1 lemon, halved
1 tablespoon kosher salt
1 teaspoon cayenne pepper
1 celery stalk

1 tablespoon pickling spice
1 tablespoon crab seasoning
6 red bliss potatoes
1 pound spicy smoked sausage
2 ears of corn, cut in half
2 pounds large shrimp, in the shell
1 dozen little neck clams, cleaned and in the shell

1. Place all ingredients, except corn, shrimp and clams, into the pressure cooker; secure lid.

2. Set pressure cooker to VEGGIE and timer to 10 minutes.

3. When cooking is complete, add remaining ingredients to the pressure cooker; secure lid.

4. Set pressure cooker to VEGGIE and timer to 5 minutes.

5. When cooking is complete, serve immediately.

(**Deb's Tip:**
I like to place my pressure cooker in the middle of the table, have bibs for all my guests and serve with drawn butter.)

rich beef stock

makes 4 cups

INGREDIENTS

4 pounds beef rib bones
1 tablespoon extra-virgin olive oil
1 tablespoon sea salt
1 teaspoon freshly ground pepper
1 medium sweet onion, quartered
4 ounces button mushrooms
5 garlic cloves

1 cup red wine
5 cups water
2 celery stalks
1 carrot, peeled
2 sprigs fresh thyme
2 tablespoons tomato paste

1. Preheat oven to 350 degrees.

2. Place the rib bones into an oven-safe skillet.

3. Add the oil, salt and pepper to the skillet; toss.

4. Add the onions, mushrooms and garlic to the skillet; toss again.

5. Place the skillet in the oven and roast for 1 hour.

6. Transfer the skillet contents to the pressure cooker.

7. Add the wine to deglaze the skillet; scrape up all the little bits from the bottom of the skillet then transfer the skillet contents to the pressure cooker.

8. Add remaining ingredients to the pressure cooker; secure lid.

9. Set pressure cooker to MEAT and timer to 45 minutes.

10. When cooking is complete, strain the stock through a fine sieve into a container with a lid.

11. Cover and refrigerate for 3 hours.

12. Remove hardened fat from the top of the stock before using.

13. Stock will keep refrigerated for up to one week or frozen for up to 6 months.

fish stock

makes 4 cups

INGREDIENTS

2 pounds snapper or grouper fish heads
1 medium onion, quartered
1 celery stalk
1 small carrot
2 sprigs thyme
6 whole peppercorns
½ tablespoon kosher salt
4 cups water

1. Place all ingredients into the pressure cooker; secure lid.

2. Set pressure cooker to MEAT and timer to 15 minutes.

3. When cooking is complete, strain stock using a colander.

4. Cover and refrigerate.

5. Stock will keep refrigerated for up to 7 days.

Deb's Tip:
Use an airtight container when storing stocks.

vegetable stock

makes 5 cups

INGREDIENTS

4 medium onions, unpeeled and quartered
4 medium carrots, cut into 2-inch pieces
3 medium potatoes, halved
2 medium parsnips or turnips, cut into 2-inch pieces
1 small head of cabbage, cut into wedges
1 tablespoon extra-virgin olive oil
½ tablespoon salt
¼ teaspoon black pepper
8 cups water
1 sprig rosemary
1 tablespoon fresh oregano, chopped

1. Preheat oven to 350 degrees.

2. Place all vegetables on a roasting pan; drizzle with oil and sprinkle with salt and pepper.

3. Place pan in the oven and let roast for 30 minutes.

4. When roasting is complete, transfer pan contents and remaining ingredients to the pressure cooker; secure lid.

5. Set pressure cooker to SOUP and timer to 20 minutes.

6. When cooking is complete, strain the stock using a colander.

7. Cover and refrigerate.

8. Stock will keep refrigerated for up to 5 days.

rich chicken stock

makes 4 cups

INGREDIENTS

2 pounds whole chicken wings, raw
1 tablespoon extra-virgin olive oil
1 tablespoon sea salt
1 teaspoon black pepper
1 teaspoon poultry seasoning
1 leek (white part only), split
1 parsnip, peeled, cut into 1-inch pieces

3 garlic cloves
1 cup white wine
3 cups water
2 celery stalks, cut into 2-inch pieces
1 teaspoon turmeric powder
2 sprigs fresh thyme

1. Preheat oven to 350 degrees.

2. Place the chicken wings in a large oven-proof skillet.

3. Add the oil, salt, pepper and poultry seasoning to the skillet; toss.

4. Add leek, parsnip and garlic to the skillet; toss again.

5. Place the skillet in the oven and roast for 1 hour.

6. Transfer the skillet contents to the pressure cooker.

7. Add the wine to deglaze the skillet; scrape up all the little bits from the bottom of the pan and pour it into the pressure cooker.

8. Add remaining ingredients to the pressure cooker; secure lid.

9. Set pressure cooker to MEAT and timer to 30 minutes.

10. When cooking is complete, strain the stock through a fine sieve into a container with a lid.

11. Cover and refrigerate for 3 hours.

12. Remove hardened fat from the top of the stock.

13. Stock will keep refrigerated for up to one week or frozen for up to 6 months.

chicken soup

makes 6 servings

INGREDIENTS

1 (5 pound) whole chicken
4 cups water
2 teaspoons sea salt
1 teaspoon turmeric powder
½ teaspoon black pepper
1 sprig fresh thyme
1 leek (white part only), halved
2 garlic cloves
2 celery stalks, cut into 2-inch pieces
2 whole carrots, peeled and cut into 2-inch pieces
½ cup dry egg noodles
1 tablespoon flat leaf parsley, chopped

1. Place all ingredients, except celery, carrots, noodles and parsley, into the pressure cooker; secure lid.

2. Set pressure cooker to SOUP and timer to 30 minutes.

3. When cooking is complete, strain the pressure cooker contents through a sieve into a container.

4. Refrigerate the stock for 30 minutes.

5. Remove the chicken meat from the bones, place the meat back into the pressure cooker and discard the bones.

6. Remove the stock from the refrigerator, discard the hardened fat from the top then pour it back into the pressure cooker.

7. Add remaining ingredients to the pressure cooker; secure lid.

8. Set pressure cooker to SOUP and timer to 5 minutes.

9. When cooking is complete, serve immediately.

greek lemon chicken soup

makes 6 servings

INGREDIENTS

6 cups chicken stock
2 boneless, skinless chicken breasts
1 teaspoon salt
1 teaspoon freshly ground pepper
½ teaspoon turmeric powder
1 bay leaf
1 teaspoon lemon zest
1 medium onion, chopped

1 celery stalk, sliced
1 carrot, peeled and sliced
¼ cup quinoa, rinsed
½ cup lemon juice
2 large eggs, beaten
1 egg yolk, beaten
2 tablespoons mint leaves, chopped

1. Place all ingredients, except quinoa, lemon juice, eggs, yolk and mint leaves, into the pressure cooker; secure lid.

2. Set pressure cooker to MEAT and timer to 20 minutes.

3. When cooking is complete, pour the pressure cooker contents through a strainer, separating the stock from the chicken and vegetables.

4. Pour the stock into the pressure cooker.

5. Discard all vegetables and chop the chicken; set aside.

6. Add the quinoa to the pressure cooker.

7. Set pressure cooker to RICE and timer to 5 minutes; cook with the lid off.

8. When cooking is complete, combine the lemon juice, eggs and yolk in a bowl; whisk well.

9. Ladle 1/4 cup of hot stock into the egg mixture; whisk well.

10. Drizzle the egg mixture into the pressure cooker while continuously whisking.

11. Add the chicken and mint to the pressure cooker.

12. Cook for an additional 3 minutes before serving.

swiss chard white bean stew

makes 4 to 6 servings

INGREDIENTS

1 bunch Swiss chard, washed and cut into 1-inch pieces
1 medium sweet onion, diced
3 garlic cloves, sliced
1 pound red bliss potatoes, washed and diced
1 cup white beans, cooked
2 sprigs fresh thyme
1 cup vegetable stock
1 teaspoon salt
½ teaspoon freshly ground pepper

1. Place all ingredients into the pressure cooker; secure lid.

2. Set pressure cooker to VEGGIE and timer to 10 minutes.

3. When cooking is complete, remove the thyme sprigs and serve.

(Deb's Tip:
Serve this delicious stew topped with grated Parmesan cheese and a slice of crusty bread.)

pork & apple stew

makes 4 servings

INGREDIENTS

2 tablespoons extra-virgin olive oil
1 pork loin roast (1½ pounds), cut into 2-inch chunks
1 teaspoon salt
1 teaspoon freshly ground pepper
½ teaspoon fennel seeds
1 teaspoon rosemary leaves
1 cup chicken stock
2 Granny Smith apples, peeled, cored, sliced and divided
1 cup purple cabbage, shredded
6 red bliss potatoes, washed and halved

Deb's Tip:
Serve with a touch
of cider vinegar.

1. Preheat oil in a large skillet over medium-high heat.

2. Season the pork with salt, pepper, fennel and rosemary.

3. Add the pork to the skillet and sear for 2 minutes on each side.

4. Transfer the pork to the pressure cooker.

5. Add the chicken stock to deglaze the skillet; scrape up all the little bits from the bottom of the skillet then transfer the skillet contents to the pressure cooker.

6. Add half of the apples to the pressure cooker; secure lid.

7. Set pressure cooker to STEW and timer to 30 minutes.

8. When cooking is complete add the cabbage, potatoes and remaining apples to the pressure cooker; secure lid.

9. Set pressure cooker to VEGGIE and timer to 5 minutes.

10. When cooking is complete, serve immediately.

beef bourguignon

makes 6 servings

INGREDIENTS

2 tablespoons extra-virgin olive oil
2-pound chuck roast, cut into ½-inch pieces
1 teaspoon sea salt
½ teaspoon freshly ground pepper
8 ounces baby portobello mushrooms, sliced
1 cup beef stock
1 cup pearl onions
4 garlic cloves
3 sprigs fresh thyme
2 tablespoons black currant jelly
¼ cup crushed tomatoes
2 carrots, peeled and sliced into 2-inch pieces

1. Preheat oil in a large skillet over medium-high heat.

2. Season the meat with salt and pepper.

3. Place the meat into the skillet; sear each side until browned.

4. Add the mushrooms to the skillet and cook for 3 minutes; stir occasionally.

5. Add the stock to deglaze the skillet; scrape up all the little bits from the bottom of the skillet then transfer the skillet contents to the pressure cooker.

6. Add remaining ingredients to the pressure cooker; secure lid.

7. Set pressure cooker to STEW and timer to 30 minutes.

8. When cooking is complete, discard the thyme sprigs and serve.

spicy bulgur pilaf

makes 6 servings

INGREDIENTS

1 medium onion, chopped
1 garlic clove, sliced
1 cup bulgur
½ teaspoon turmeric powder
½ teaspoon cumin seeds
1½ cups chicken stock
1 tablespoon lemon zest
½ cup black olives
¼ cup lemon juice
1 tablespoon fresh cilantro leaves, chopped

1. Place all ingredients, except cilantro, into the pressure cooker; secure lid.

2. Set pressure cooker to RICE and timer to 6 minutes.

3. When cooking is complete, fluff using a fork, top with cilantro and serve.

Deb's Tip:
Bulgur is a healthy and delicious substitute for rice.

macaroni & cheese

makes 4 to 6 servings

INGREDIENTS

2½ cups dry elbow macaroni
2 cups chicken stock
1 cup heavy cream
1 teaspoon salt
1 teaspoon freshly ground pepper
1 tablespoon butter
½ cup whole milk
1½ cups cheddar cheese, shredded
1½ cups mozzarella cheese, shredded

1. Place macaroni, stock, cream, salt and pepper into the pressure cooker; secure lid.

2. Set pressure cooker to RICE and timer to 8 minutes.

3. When cooking is complete, add remaining ingredients to the pressure cooker and stir until creamy.

4. Serve immediately.

buffalo chicken
mac & cheese

makes 4 to 6 servings

INGREDIENTS

6 frozen chicken tenders
3 cups dry rigatoni pasta
3 cups chicken stock
1 small onion, chopped
2 celery stalks, chopped
1 large carrot, peeled and chopped
⅔ cup buffalo wing sauce
1 tablespoon ranch seasoning (optional)
½ cup cream cheese
1 cup sharp cheddar cheese, shredded
1 cup Swiss cheese, shredded
½ cup gorgonzola cheese, crumbled and divided
1 cup cheddar French fried onions, crushed

1. Place the chicken, pasta, stock, onions, celery, carrots, wing sauce and ranch seasoning into the pressure cooker; secure lid.

2. Set pressure cooker to RICE and timer to 10 minutes.

3. When cooking is complete, add the cream cheese to the pressure cooker; stir until dissolved.

4. Add the cheddar cheese, Swiss cheese and 1/4 cup gorgonzola cheese to the pressure cooker; stir until dissolved.

5. Top with French fried onions and remaining gorgonzola before serving.

deb's famous meaty pasta

makes 6 servings

INGREDIENTS

1 pound frozen ground beef
3 cups dry penne or ziti pasta
2½ cups beef stock
3 cups pasta sauce
1 teaspoon salt
½ teaspoon freshly ground pepper
1 teaspoon Italian seasoning
½ teaspoon garlic powder
½ cup Mozzarella cheese, shredded

1. Place all ingredients into the pressure cooker; secure lid.

2. Set pressure cooker to MEAT and timer to 20 minutes.

3. When cooking is complete, break the meat apart using a rubber spatula, stir and serve.

artichokes in lemon dill

makes 4 to 6 servings

INGREDIENTS

3 whole artichokes
1 cup white wine
½ cup chicken stock
Juice and zest from 1 lemon
2 sprigs fresh dill
2 garlic cloves

1. Place the artichokes, stem-side up, into the pressure cooker.

2. Add remaining ingredients to the pressure cooker; secure lid.

3. Set pressure cooker to VEGGIE and timer to 15 minutes.

4. When cooking is complete, serve hot with some broth on the side.

Deb's Tip:
Chill and serve topped with
your favorite vinaigrette.

sweet beets & carrots

makes 4 to 6 servings

INGREDIENTS

1 pound beets, golden and/or red, peeled and quartered
1 pound carrots, yellow and/or orange, peeled and sliced
½ cup rich chicken stock (see recipe on page 40)
½ teaspoon salt
½ teaspoon freshly ground pepper
1 teaspoon lemon zest
1 sprig fresh thyme
2 tablespoons butter

1. Place all ingredients into the pressure cooker; secure lid.

2. Set pressure cooker to VEGGIE and timer to 10 minutes.

3. When cooking is complete, remove the thyme sprig and serve.

beet greens with smoked turkey wings

makes 4 to 6 servings

INGREDIENTS

3 pounds beet tops, washed and cut into 2-inch pieces
1 smoked turkey wing, meat chopped into ½-inch chunks
1 small sweet onion, chopped
½ cup chicken stock
½ teaspoon salt
½ teaspoon cayenne pepper
Pinch of sugar

1. Place all ingredients, including the turkey wing bone, into the pressure cooker; stir then close the lid.

2. Set pressure cooker to VEGGIE and timer to 10 minutes.

3. When cooking is complete, discard the bone and serve.

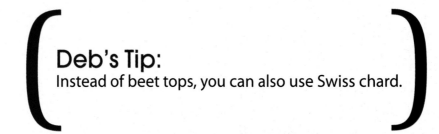

(Deb's Tip:
Instead of beet tops, you can also use Swiss chard.)

buttery corn on the cob

makes 4 to 6 servings

INGREDIENTS

6 ears of corn, husked
½ cup water
1 teaspoon salt
½ teaspoon sugar
3 tablespoons butter

1. Place all ingredients into the pressure cooker; secure lid.

2. Set pressure cooker to VEGGIE and timer to 6 minutes.

3. When cooking is complete, stir and serve.

Deb's Tip:
Add some more salt and butter if desired.

spaghetti squash

makes 4 servings

INGREDIENTS

1 large spaghetti squash, seeds removed and cut horizontally
2 tablespoons butter, divided
¼ teaspoon kosher salt
¼ teaspoon black pepper
2 cups water

1. Place 1 tablespoon of butter on each squash half.

2. Sprinkle salt and pepper over the squash.

3. Pour the water into the pressure cooker.

4. Fit the pressure cooker with the stainless rack and place the squash on the rack; secure lid.

5. Set pressure cooker to VEGGIE and timer to 30 minutes.

6. When cooking is complete, serve immediately.

lemon dill green beans

makes 6 servings

INGREDIENTS

2 pounds green beans, stems trimmed
¼ cup chicken stock
¼ cup lemon juice
1 teaspoon lemon zest
2 garlic cloves, minced
1 shallot, minced
½ teaspoon salt
½ teaspoon freshly ground pepper
1 tablespoon extra-virgin olive oil
1 teaspoon fresh dill, chopped

1. Place all ingredients into the pressure cooker; secure lid.

2. Set pressure cooker to VEGGIE and timer to 5 minutes.

3. When cooking is complete, serve immediately.

braised purple cabbage

makes 4 to 6 servings

INGREDIENTS

1 head of purple cabbage, sliced
3 apples, cored and quartered
1 large onion, sliced
2 cups beef stock
1 teaspoon sugar
1 teaspoon salt
½ teaspoon freshly ground pepper
1 tablespoon balsamic vinegar
1 teaspoon caraway seeds

1. Place all ingredients, except caraway seeds, into the pressure cooker; secure lid.

2. Set pressure cooker to VEGGIE and timer to 20 minutes.

3. When cooking is complete, add caraway seeds and serve.

brussels sprouts with pearl onions

makes 4 servings

INGREDIENTS

1½ pounds Brussels sprouts, trimmed
1 bag (10 ounces) frozen pearl onions
1 cup beef stock
1 teaspoon salt
½ teaspoon freshly ground pepper
1 sprig fresh thyme

1. Place all ingredients into the pressure cooker; secure lid.

2. Set pressure cooker to VEGGIE and timer to 8 minutes.

3. When cooking is complete, remove thyme sprig and serve.

(Deb's Tip:
I love to serve this with a side
of horseradish sauce.)

mashed potatoes with rutabaga

makes 4 servings

INGREDIENTS

6 Yukon Gold potatoes, peeled and halved
½ cup rutabaga, peeled and diced into 1-inch cubes
1 cup chicken stock
1 teaspoon salt
½ teaspoon freshly ground pepper
2 tablespoons heavy cream
2 tablespoons butter

1. Place all ingredients, except cream and butter, into the pressure cooker; secure lid.

2. Set pressure cooker to VEGGIE and timer to 10 minutes.

3. When cooking is complete, drain the potatoes.

4. Add cream and butter to the potatoes and mash using a potato masher.

5. Serve immediately.

hummus

makes 6 to 8 servings

INGREDIENTS

1 cup dried garbanzo beans
Water to soak the beans
1 teaspoon baking soda
1 lemon, juice and zest
2 garlic cloves, minced
1 teaspoon cumin
3 teaspoons salt
½ teaspoon cayenne pepper
5 cups water
2 tablespoons tahini paste
1 cup extra-virgin olive oil

(**Deb's Tip:**
Great with warm pita bread.)

1. Place the garbanzo beans into a bowl; add enough water to cover the beans then add the baking soda and let soak for 1 hour.

2. Rinse the beans then transfer them to the pressure cooker.

3. Add lemon juice, zest, garlic, cumin, salt, cayenne pepper and 5 cups of water to the pressure cooker; secure lid.

4. Set pressure cooker to MEAT and timer to 30 minutes.

5. When cooking is complete, drain the beans.

6. Transfer the beans to a food processor fitted with a metal chopping blade then add the tahini paste.

7. While processing, slowly add the oil to create an emulsion and process to desired consistency.

8. Transfer hummus to a plate and serve.

parsnip purée with shallots

makes 4 servings

INGREDIENTS

2 pounds parsnips, peeled and cut into 2-inch pieces
1 shallot, minced
⅓ cup chicken stock
½ teaspoon salt
½ teaspoon freshly ground pepper
2 ounces cream cheese

1. Place all ingredients, except cream cheese, into the pressure cooker; secure lid.

2. Set pressure cooker to VEGGIE and timer to 7 minutes.

3. When cooking is complete, strain the parsnips then place them into a food processor.

4. Add the cream cheese to the food processor and purée until smooth.

5. Serve immediately.

wolf's warm potato salad

makes 4 servings

POTATO INGREDIENTS

1 pound fingerling potatoes, washed
3 garlic cloves, sliced
3 sprigs fresh parsley
2 teaspoons salt
1 cup water

MARINADE INGREDIENTS

1 cup champagne vinegar
¼ cup peanut oil
1½ teaspoons kosher salt
½ teaspoon black pepper
3 tablespoons sugar
1 tablespoon fresh thyme leaves, chopped
1 small sweet onion, cut into ¼-inch chunks

1. Place the potato ingredients into the pressure cooker; secure lid.

2. Set pressure cooker to VEGGIE and timer to 6 minutes.

3. While cooking, combine all marinade ingredients in a bowl; stir.

4. When cooking is complete, strain the potatoes and let them cool for 20 minutes.

5. Slice the potatoes into ¼-inch thick slices then toss them in the marinade.

6. Let potatoes rest for an additional 20 minutes before serving.

thai chicken curry

makes 4 to 6 servings

INGREDIENTS

2 cups chicken stock
1 medium onion, diced
3 garlic cloves, sliced
1 tablespoon fresh ginger, sliced
2 tablespoons Thai red curry paste
1 tablespoon lime zest
2 tablespoons fish sauce
2 pounds boneless chicken tenders
2 tablespoons brown sugar
1 red bell pepper, julienned
1 can (13.5 ounces) light coconut milk
1 can (8 ounces) bamboo shoots
2 tablespoons fresh cilantro leaves, chopped
Green onions, chopped

1. Place all ingredients, except green onions, into the pressure cooker; secure lid.

2. Set pressure cooker to SOUP and timer to 10 minutes.

3. When cooking is complete, top with green onions and serve.

Deb's Tip:
Serve over hot jasmine rice.

coq au vin

makes 6 servings

INGREDIENTS

1 whole chicken, cut into pieces
1 tablespoon flour
1 teaspoon salt
½ teaspoon freshly ground pepper
2 bacon strips, diced
2 tablespoons butter
8 boiler onions, peeled
1 pound whole mushrooms
2 sprigs thyme
2 cups dry red wine
1 cup chicken stock
1 teaspoon sugar

1. Rub the chicken with flour, salt and pepper.

2. In a skillet over medium heat, cook bacon until crisp.

3. Add the butter to the skillet and let it melt.

4. Add the chicken pieces to the skillet and cook until golden brown.

5. Transfer the skillet contents and remaining ingredients to the pressure cooker; secure lid.

6. Set pressure cooker to STEW and timer to 40 minutes.

7. When cooking is complete, transfer the chicken, onions and mushrooms to a platter.

8. With the lid off, set pressure cooker to STEW again and let the liquid reduce for 10 minutes.

9. Ladle sauce over the chicken and serve.

moroccan chicken

makes 4 to 6 servings

INGREDIENTS

3 pounds skinless, bone-in chicken pieces
2 tablespoons extra-virgin olive oil
1 teaspoon salt
1 teaspoon cumin seeds
1 teaspoon nigella seeds (optional)
1 cup chicken stock
1 medium onion, sliced
3 saffron strands
1 teaspoon turmeric powder
1 tablespoon lemon zest
¼ cup lemon juice
12 black olives, pitted
2 tablespoons fresh cilantro, chopped

1. Pat the chicken dry using paper towels.

2. Preheat the oil in a sauté pan over medium-high heat.

3. Place the chicken pieces into the pan; season with salt, cumin and nigella seeds.

4. Cook the chicken for 3 minutes on each side or until browned.

5. Transfer the chicken to the pressure cooker.

6. Add the stock to the pan; scrape up all the little bits from the bottom of the pan then transfer the pan contents to the pressure cooker.

7. Add remaining ingredients, except cilantro, to the pressure cooker; secure the lid.

8. Set pressure cooker to MEAT and timer to 20 minutes.

9. When cooking is complete, top the chicken with cilantro and serve.

spicy chipotle chicken burrito

makes 4 to 6 servings

INGREDIENTS

4 boneless, skinless chicken breasts, chopped into 1-inch pieces
1 cup chicken stock
2 whole chipotles in adobo sauce
1 teaspoon cumin seeds
1 teaspoon salt
1 teaspoon freshly ground pepper
1 teaspoon sugar
1 can (10 ounces) Mexican tomatoes with green chilies and lime
1 cup jasmine rice
1 cup black beans, cooked
½ cup cheddar cheese, shredded
2 tablespoons fresh cilantro, chopped
6 (12-inches each) flour tortillas

1. Place all ingredients, except tortillas, into the pressure cooker; secure lid.

2. Set pressure cooker to RICE and timer to 10 minutes.

3. When cooking is complete, assemble the burritos by spooning the chicken mixture down the center of each tortilla and rolling them into burritos.

(Deb's Tip:
To make them even more delicious, serve the burritos with lettuce, avocado and sour cream.)

chicken tacos

makes 4 servings

INGREDIENTS

3 frozen boneless, skinless chicken breasts
1 box taco dinner kit
1 cup chicken stock
1 teaspoon lime zest
1 cup lettuce, shredded
1 tomato, diced
3 green onions, chopped
½ cup cheddar cheese, shredded
½ cup sour cream

1. Place the chicken, taco seasoning from the dinner kit, stock and lime zest into the pressure cooker; secure lid.

2. Set pressure cooker to MEAT and timer to 20 minutes.

3. When cooking is complete, shred the chicken using 2 forks.

4. Make a large platter with lettuce, tomatoes, green onions, cheese, sour cream, chicken, taco sauce and shells.

5. Let everyone dress their tacos the way they like.

chicken enchilada casserole

makes 4 to 6 servings

INGREDIENTS

2 pounds boneless, skinless chicken breasts
1 can (4 ounces) green chiles, chopped
1 envelope taco seasoning
1 cup chicken stock
1 can (18.6 ounces) tortilla soup
12 tortilla chips
1 can (10 ounces) enchilada sauce
1 cup colby and cheddar cheese blend, shredded
3 green onions, chopped
Sour cream

1. Place chicken, chiles, taco seasoning, stock and tortilla soup into the pressure cooker; secure lid.

2. Set pressure cooker to STEW and timer to 15 minutes.

3. When cooking is complete, add the tortilla chips, enchilada sauce and cheese; stir and secure lid.

4. Set pressure cooker to VEGGIE and timer to 3 minutes.

5. When cooking is complete, garnish with green onions and sour cream.

6. Serve immediately.

chicken marsala

makes 4 servings

INGREDIENTS

4 frozen boneless, skinless chicken breasts
1 cup mushrooms, sliced
1 shallot, sliced
½ cup chicken stock
½ cup marsala wine
1 sprig thyme
1 teaspoon salt
½ teaspoon freshly ground pepper
1 envelope brown gravy mix

1. Place all ingredients into the pressure cooker; secure lid.

2. Set pressure cooker to MEAT and timer to 20 minutes.

3. When cooking is complete, remove the thyme sprig.

4. Transfer the chicken to a platter, pour sauce over the chicken and serve.

chicken & yellow rice

makes 8 servings

INGREDIENTS

1 bag (16 ounces) yellow rice
4 boneless, skinless chicken breasts, cubed
2 tablespoons extra-virgin olive oil
1 teaspoon salt
½ teaspoon freshly ground pepper
4 cups water
1 cup frozen peas
½ cup Spanish olives

1. Place all ingredients, except olives, into the pressure cooker; secure lid.

2. Set pressure cooker to RICE and timer to 20 minutes.

3. When cooking is complete, add the olives, stir and serve.

stuffed turkey breast

makes 4 to 6 servings

INGREDIENTS

2 pounds turkey breast tenderloins, butterflied
½ teaspoon salt
¼ teaspoon poultry seasoning
1 box (6 ounces) turkey flavored stuffing mix
½ cup dried cherries
Toothpicks
1 cup chicken stock
1 envelope turkey gravy

1. Sprinkle turkey with salt and poultry seasoning.

2. Prepare stuffing mix according to package directions then add the dried cherries to the stuffing.

3. Divide the stuffing between the tenderloins and place the mixture in the center of each tenderloin.

4. Roll tenderloins to cover the stuffing then secure with toothpicks.

5. Add the stock and gravy envelope content to the pressure cooker.

6. Place turkey, toothpick-side down, into the pressure cooker; secure lid.

7. Set pressure cooker to MEAT and timer to 20 minutes.

8. When cooking is complete, transfer the turkey to a cutting board.

9. Remove toothpicks, slice the turkey into 1-inch rounds and serve with gravy.

(Deb's Tip:
Try dried cranberries instead of the cherries.)

turkey pot roast

makes 4 to 6 servings

INGREDIENTS

1 (4 pound) boneless turkey breast, rinsed
½ teaspoon sea salt
½ teaspoon freshly ground pepper
½ teaspoon poultry seasoning
1 tablespoon extra-virgin olive oil
1 medium onion, quartered
¼ cup mushrooms, sliced

½ cup amber beer
½ cup chicken stock
1 tablespoon tomato paste
2 celery stalks, diced
2 sprigs fresh thyme
4 red bliss potatoes, halved
3 carrots, peeled, cut into 2-inch pieces

1. Pat the turkey breast dry using paper towels.

2. Rub turkey breast with salt, pepper and poultry seasoning.

3. Preheat oil in a large skillet over medium heat.

4. Gently place the turkey breast into the skillet; sear until all sides are golden brown.

5. Transfer the turkey breast to the pressure cooker.

6. Place the onions and mushrooms into the skillet; cook for 2 minutes.

7. Add the beer and stock to deglaze the skillet; scrape up all the little bits from the bottom of the skillet then transfer the skillet contents to the pressure cooker.

8. Add the tomato paste, celery and thyme to the pressure cooker; stir then secure lid.

9. Set pressure cooker to MEAT and timer to 45 minutes.

10. When cooking is complete, carefully remove the lid and add remaining ingredients to the pressure cooker; secure lid.

11. Set pressure cooker to VEGGIE and timer to 10 minutes.

12. When cooking is complete, remove the thyme sprigs and serve.

pork chops l'orange

makes 4 servings

INGREDIENTS

4 bone-in pork chops, 1-inch thick
1 tablespoon extra-virgin olive oil
½ teaspoon salt
½ cup chicken stock
¼ cup brown sugar
1 teaspoon cider vinegar
1 teaspoon freshly grated ginger
½ teaspoon dry mustard
1 teaspoon dried marjoram
1 teaspoon orange zest
1 sprig fresh thyme
½ teaspoon black pepper
2 oranges, peeled and sectioned

1. Preheat a large skillet over medium-high heat.

2. Rub the pork chops with olive oil then season with salt.

3. Place the pork chops into the skillet and sear for 2 minutes on each side.

4. Transfer the pork chops to the pressure cooker.

5. Add the chicken stock to deglaze the skillet; scrape up all the little bits from the bottom of the skillet then transfer the skillet contents to the pressure cooker.

6. Add remaining ingredients to the pressure cooker; secure lid.

7. Set pressure cooker to MEAT and timer to 20 minutes.

8. When cooking is complete, serve immediately.

asian style baby back ribs

makes 2 to 4 servings

INGREDIENTS

1 full slab baby back ribs
½ cup chicken stock
2 tablespoons fresh ginger, sliced
1 medium onion, quartered
2 garlic cloves
2 tablespoons sesame oil
2 tablespoons soy sauce
2 tablespoons rice wine vinegar
2 tablespoons brown sugar

1. Place all ingredients, except brown sugar, into the pressure cooker; secure lid.

2. Set pressure cooker to MEAT and timer to 25 minutes.

3. When cooking is complete, transfer the ribs to a broiler pan, bone-side down.

4. Preheat the broiler on high.

5. To reduce the liquid in the pressure cooker, set it to RICE and timer to 10 minutes; let cook with the lid off until the liquid turns into a syrup-like glaze.

6. While the liquid is reducing, rub the meat side of the ribs with brown sugar and place the ribs under the broiler for 10 minutes or until golden brown.

7. Pour some glaze over the ribs and serve with additional glaze on the side.

Deb's Tip:
If you don't have fresh ginger, the bottled variety commonly found in the sushi section of your supermarket is a perfect substitute.

osso buco

makes 4 servings

INGREDIENTS

2 pounds meaty veal shanks
½ cup onions, diced
½ cup celery, diced
½ cup parsnips, diced
2 garlic cloves, minced
1 teaspoon salt
½ teaspoon freshly ground pepper
½ cup vermouth
1 can (14½ ounces) petite diced tomatoes
1 sprig thyme
1 teaspoon orange zest
1 cup beef stock

1. Place all ingredients into the pressure cooker; secure lid.

2. Set pressure cooker to MEAT and timer to 40 minutes.

3. When cooking is complete, remove the thyme sprig then transfer the veal to a platter.

4. With the lid off, set pressure cooker to MEAT and let the sauce reduce for 10 minutes.

5. Using a blender, purée the sauce, pour it over the veal and serve.

moroccan lamb shanks

makes 4 servings

INGREDIENTS

2 tablespoons extra-virgin olive oil
4 (1 pound each) lamb shanks
½ teaspoon salt
½ teaspoon freshly ground pepper
½ cup dry red wine
½ cup chicken stock
2 tablespoons tomato paste
½ cup carrots, diced
1 shallot, minced
3 garlic cloves, minced
½ teaspoon cumin seeds
½ teaspoon coriander seeds
½ teaspoon pumpkin pie spice
1 can (16.5 ounces) petite diced tomatoes
2 tablespoons fresh cilantro, chopped

1. Preheat oil in a large skillet over medium-high heat.

2. Season the lamb shanks with salt and pepper.

3. Add the lamb to the skillet and sear each shank on all sides until browned.

4. Transfer the lamb shanks to the pressure cooker.

5. Drain the fat from the skillet.

6. Add the red wine to deglaze the skillet; scrape up all the little bits from the bottom of the skillet then transfer the skillet contents to the pressure cooker.

7. Add remaining ingredients, except cilantro, to the pressure cooker; secure lid.

8. Set pressure cooker to MEAT and timer to 60 minutes.

9. When cooking is complete, top with cilantro and serve.

meatballs for spaghetti

makes 6 to 8 servings

MEATBALL INGREDIENTS

1½ cups fresh breadcrumbs
4 cups beef stock, divided
1 pound ground chuck
½ pound ground pork
3 garlic cloves, minced
1 small onion, minced
¾ cup Romano cheese, grated
1 teaspoon salt
½ teaspoon freshly ground pepper
2 large eggs, beaten

SAUCE INGREDIENTS

4 tablespoons extra-virgin olive oil
4 tablespoons tomato paste
2 cans (28 ounces each) Italian tomatoes
3 garlic cloves, minced
1 small onion, minced
1 teaspoon dry oregano
1 teaspoon dried basil

1. In a bowl, soak the breadcrumbs in 2 cups of beef stock.

2. Pour remaining stock into the pressure cooker and set it to MEAT.

3. Add remaining meatball ingredients to the breadcrumbs; mix then form into 2-inch meatballs.

4. Place the meatballs into the pressure cooker; secure lid.

5. Set pressure cooker to MEAT and timer to 20 minutes.

6. When cooking is complete, transfer the meatballs to a platter then pour the stock into a separate bowl and skim off the fat.

7. Dissolve tomato paste in the strained stock then pour it into the pressure cooker.

8. Add remaining sauce ingredients and meatballs to the pressure cooker; secure lid.

9. Set pressure cooker to STEW and timer to 15 minutes.

10. When cooking is complete, serve over spaghetti.

stuffed flank steak

makes 4 servings

INGREDIENTS

2 pounds flank steak
1 bell pepper, cut into strips
1 small onion, cut into strips
3 slices Mozzarella cheese
Butcher's twine
1 tablespoon extra-virgin olive oil
1 teaspoon Italian seasoning
1 teaspoon salt
½ teaspoon black pepper
2 cups beef stock
1 can (14½ ounces) Italian seasoned stewed tomatoes

Deb's Tip:
Serve with rice or pasta.

1. Open the steak and place the peppers, onions and cheese on the steak.

2. Roll up the steak then tie it with twine.

3. Rub the roll with oil, Italian seasoning, salt and pepper.

4. Add roll, stock and stewed tomatoes to the pressure cooker; secure lid.

5. Set pressure cooker to MEAT and timer to 45 minutes.

6. When cooking is complete, remove the roll, discard the twine then cut the steak into ½-inch slices.

7. Place steak slices on a platter, top with sauce from the pressure cooker and serve.

stuffed cabbage rolls

makes 4 servings

INGREDIENTS

½ pound ground chuck
½ pound ground pork
1 small onion, chopped
½ cup white rice, uncooked
½ teaspoon thyme leaves
1 cup Swiss cheese, shredded
8 large cabbage leaves
Toothpicks
1 cup beef stock
1 can (15 ounces) tomato sauce
1 teaspoon sugar
1 teaspoon oregano
½ teaspoon garlic powder
1 tablespoon cider vinegar

1. In a bowl, combine the meats, onions, rice, thyme and cheese; mix well.

2. Place ⅓ cup of the meat mixture onto each cabbage leaf; fold in the sides then roll up.

3. Secure rolls with toothpicks then place them into the pressure cooker.

4. In a bowl, combine remaining ingredients then pour them into the pressure cooker; secure lid.

5. Set pressure cooker to MEAT and timer to 20 minutes.

6. When cooking is complete, serve immediately.

beef short ribs

makes 4 servings

INGREDIENTS

4 beef short ribs
1 cup beef stock
1 teaspoon salt
½ teaspoon freshly ground pepper
1 leek (white part only), split
2 carrots, peeled and cut into 2-inch slices
2 celery stalks, sliced

4 garlic cloves
1 shallot, halved
2 sprigs fresh thyme
1 tablespoon Worcestershire sauce
1 teaspoon soy sauce
1 tablespoon grape jelly
1 tablespoon tomato paste

1. Place all ingredients, except jelly and tomato paste, into the pressure cooker; secure lid.

2. Set pressure cooker to MEAT and timer to 40 minutes.

3. When cooking is complete, add the jelly and tomato paste to the pressure cooker; stir then secure the lid.

4. Set pressure cooker to MEAT and timer to 20 minutes.

5. When cooking is complete, strain the pressure cooker contents through a sieve into a container; reserve the vegetables in a bowl.

6. Refrigerate the stock for 30 minutes.

7. Place the short ribs back into the pressure cooker.

8. Set pressure cooker to KEEP WARM.

9. Using a blender, purée the vegetables until smooth then place them back into the pressure cooker.

10. Remove the stock from the refrigerator, discard the hardened fat and pour it back into the pressure cooker.

11. Stir until heated then serve.

italian pot roast

makes 4 to 6 servings

INGREDIENTS

2 tablespoons extra-virgin olive oil
1 (4 pound) chuck roast
1 teaspoon salt
½ teaspoon freshly ground pepper
¼ cup dry red wine
1 cup beef stock
1 medium onion, sliced

3 garlic cloves, sliced
1 bell pepper, diced
1 teaspoon garlic powder
1 teaspoon Italian herb seasoning
1 bay leaf
1 bottle (28 ounces) pasta sauce
Pasta or polenta, cooked

1. Preheat oil in a large skillet over medium heat.

2. Season the roast with salt and pepper.

3. Add the roast to the skillet then sear for 3 minutes on each side.

4. Transfer the roast to the pressure cooker.

5. Drain the fat from the skillet.

6. Add the wine and stock to deglaze the skillet; scrape up all the little bits from the bottom of the skillet then transfer the skillet contents to the pressure cooker.

7. Add the onions, garlic, bell peppers, garlic powder, Italian seasoning and bay leaf to the pressure cooker; secure lid.

8. Set pressure cooker to MEAT and timer to 60 minutes.

9. When cooking is complete, discard the bay leaf then add the pasta sauce to the pressure cooker; secure lid.

10. Set pressure cooker to RICE and timer to 6 minutes.

11. When cooking is complete, serve over your favorite pasta or polenta.

holiday brisket with root veggies

makes 4 to 6 servings

INGREDIENTS

2 tablespoons extra-virgin olive oil
1 (3 pound) first cut brisket
1 teaspoon salt
1 teaspoon freshly ground pepper
½ cup port wine
1 cup sweet onions, sliced
1 sprig fresh thyme

4 allspice berries
1 bay leaf
1 cup beef stock
1 tablespoon tomato paste
½ cup carrots, peeled and sliced
½ cup parsnip, peeled and sliced
½ cup celery root, peeled and diced

1. Preheat oil in a large sauté pan over medium-high heat.

2. Season the brisket with salt and pepper.

3. Add the brisket to the pan and brown for 3 minutes on each side.

4. Transfer the brisket to the pressure cooker and drain the grease from the sauté pan.

5. Add the wine to deglaze the pan; scrape up all the little bits from the bottom of the pan then transfer the pan contents to the pressure cooker.

6. Add the onions, thyme, allspice berries, bay leaf, stock and tomato paste to the pressure cooker; secure lid.

7. Set pressure cooker to MEAT and timer to 60 minutes.

8. When cooking is complete, discard the thyme sprig and bay leaf.

9. Add remaining ingredients to the pressure cooker; secure lid.

10. Set pressure cooker to VEGGIE and timer to 5 minutes.

11. When cooking is complete, cut the brisket against the grain and serve.

desserts

poached pears

makes 4 servings

INGREDIENTS

1 bottle (750ml) port wine
4 Bartlett pears, peeled
3 sprigs rosemary
½ teaspoon whole peppercorns

1. Pour the wine into the pressure cooker.

2. Using a melon baller, core the bottom of each pear.

3. Cut off the bottom of each pear so they sit flat.

4. Place the pears into the pressure cooker.

5. Add the rosemary and peppercorns to the pressure cooker; secure lid.

6. Set pressure cooker to VEGGIE and timer to 10 minutes.

7. When cooking is complete, transfer the pears to a platter.

8. To reduce the liquid inside the pressure cooker, set pressure cooker to RICE and timer to 10 minutes; cook with the lid off until the liquid turns into a syrup.

9. Top the pears with syrup and serve.

(Deb's Tip:
Serve the poached pears topped with your favorite ice cream.)

lemon curd

makes 4 servings

INGREDIENTS

1¼ cups sugar
2 tablespoons lemon zest
½ cup bottled lemon juice
⅓ cup unsalted butter, cut into small pieces
4 egg yolks
3 large eggs
1 cup water

1. Process the sugar in a blender until very fine then transfer it to a 2-quart bowl.

2. Add remaining ingredients, except water, to the bowl; beat using a whisk.

3. Cover the bowl tightly in aluminum foil.

4. Pour the water into the pressure cooker.

5. Place the bowl into the pressure cooker; secure lid.

6. Set pressure cooker to RICE and timer to 13 minutes.

7. When cooking is complete, carefully remove the foil then whisk the ingredients well.

8. Refrigerate for 1 hour before serving.

coconut soup

makes 4 to 6 servings

INGREDIENTS

2 cans (13½ ounces each) light coconut milk
¼ cup small pearl tapioca
¼ cup sugar
¼ cup sweetened coconut, shredded
1 teaspoon coconut extract

1. Place coconut milk, tapioca and sugar into the pressure cooker; secure lid.

2. Set pressure cooker to RICE and timer to 6 minutes.

3. When cooking is complete, stir in remaining ingredients; let cool.

4. Pour soup into glasses and serve chilled.

(**Deb's Tip:**
You can find small pearl tapioca in most Asian supermarkets.)

creamy quinoa pudding

makes 4 servings

INGREDIENTS

1 cup quinoa, rinsed
1 cup water
1½ cups rice milk
2 tablespoons agave syrup
Pinch of salt
1 vanilla bean, split
¼ cup dried cherries

1. Place all ingredients into the pressure cooker; secure lid.

2. Set pressure cooker to RICE and timer to 12 minutes.

3. When cooking is complete, remove the vanilla bean and scrape the inside of the bean into the pudding; stir.

4. Serve immediately.

(**Deb's Tip:**
This pudding is also delicious served chilled.)

brown rice pudding

makes 6 to 8 servings

INGREDIENTS

4 cups brown rice, cooked
4 cups milk
$\frac{1}{8}$ teaspoon salt
$\frac{1}{2}$ cup sugar
1 stick cinnamon
$\frac{1}{2}$ cup golden raisins
1 tablespoon amaretto liqueur

1. Place all ingredients into the pressure cooker; stir then secure lid.

2. Set pressure cooker to RICE and timer to 6 minutes.

3. When cooking is complete, serve immediately.

chocolate cherry cordial bread pudding

makes 6 to 8 servings

INGREDIENTS

6 ounces dried cherries
2 tablespoons brandy
4 large eggs, beaten
1½ cups heavy cream
½ cup brown sugar
1 teaspoon vanilla extract
1 cup chocolate chips
1 loaf challah bread, cubed and toasted

1. In a large bowl, soak the cherries in brandy for 5 minutes.

2. Add remaining ingredients to the bowl; mix well.

3. Apply non-stick spray to the pressure cooker.

4. Transfer the bowl contents to the pressure cooker; secure lid.

5. Set pressure cooker to RICE and timer to 15 minutes.

6. When cooking is complete, serve hot or cold.

(Deb's Tip:
If you don't have brandy, just use water.)

easy flan

makes 6 servings

INGREDIENTS

½ cup sugar
1½ cups water, divided
6 custard cups, 4-ounce capacity
1 can (14 ounces) sweetened condensed milk
1 can (12 ounces) evaporated milk
2 large eggs, beaten
2 large egg yolks
1 teaspoon vanilla extract
1 teaspoon orange zest

1. Preheat stove top on high.

2. In a non-stick pan, combine sugar and ½ cup water; stir until sugar is dissolved.

3. Reduce heat to medium and let sugar mixture cook for several minutes; do not stir.

4. When the water evaporates and the sugar turns to a caramel color, remove from heat then pour the caramel into custard cups; let rest for 10 minutes.

5. Pour remaining water into the pressure cooker.

6. In a bowl, combine remaining ingredients; stir then pour into custard cups.

7. Cover each cup with aluminum foil and stack cups inside the pressure cooker; secure lid.

8. Set pressure cooker to RICE and timer to 6 minutes.

9. When cooking is complete, remove cups and chill until ready to serve.

chocolate pots de crème

makes 4 servings

INGREDIENTS

2 ounces bittersweet chocolate, finely chopped
1 cup heavy cream
1 cup whole milk
4 egg yolks
2 tablespoons sugar
½ teaspoon orange zest
⅛ teaspoon salt
1 cup water

(**Deb's Tip:**
You can also serve this dessert chilled, topped with whipped cream.)

1. Apply non-stick spray to four ½-cup ramekins; set aside.

2. Place the chocolate into a mixing bowl.

3. Pour the cream and milk into a saucepan over medium heat.

4. When the cream begins to simmer, pour it into the chocolate bowl; stir until smooth.

5. In a separate bowl, combine remaining ingredients, except water.

6. Slowly pour the chocolate mixture into the yolk mixture; mix well then divide the mixture between the ramekins.

7. Wrap each ramekin in aluminum foil.

8. Pour the water into the pressure cooker and stack the ramekins inside the pressure cooker; secure lid.

9. Set pressure cooker to VEGGIE and timer to 10 minutes.

10. When cooking is complete, remove the ramekins and let rest at room temperature for 30 minutes.

11. Remove the foil and serve.

blood orange pots de crème

makes 4 servings

INGREDIENTS

1 large egg
4 egg yolks
¼ cup sugar
1 cup heavy cream
½ cup blood orange juice
1 teaspoon lemon juice
1 teaspoon lemon zest
1 cup water

1. In a bowl, combine egg, yolks and sugar; beat for 30 seconds using a fork.

2. Add the heavy cream, juices and zest to the bowl; whisk until the sugar is dissolved.

3. Strain the custard through a sieve.

4. Divide the custard between four ½-cup ramekins.

5. Wrap the ramekins tightly in aluminum foil.

6. Pour the water into the pressure cooker.

7. Place the ramekins into the pressure cooker; secure lid.

8. Set pressure cooker to VEGGIE and timer to 5 minutes.

9. When cooking is complete, remove the foil and chill for at least 30 minutes before serving.

orange upside down cake

makes 6 servings

INGREDIENTS

2 tablespoons unsalted butter
2 tablespoons brown sugar
1 teaspoon maple syrup
1 large orange, sliced into thin rings
1½ cups unbleached all purpose flour
1 cup sugar
1 teaspoon baking powder
1 teaspoon baking soda

1 teaspoon ground cinnamon
½ teaspoon allspice
½ cup safflower oil
1 cup carrots, shredded
1 cup applesauce
1 teaspoon vanilla extract
½ cup raisins
¼ cup chopped pecans (optional)

1. Place the butter into the pressure cooker.

2. Set pressure cooker to RICE and let butter melt with the lid off.

3. Add the brown sugar and syrup to the pressure cooker; stir until smooth.

4. Turn off the pressure cooker then top the sugar mixture with layers of orange rings.

5. In a large bowl, combine flour, sugar, baking powder, baking soda, cinnamon and allspice; mix well.

6. In a separate bowl, combine oil, carrots, applesauce and vanilla; mix well.

7. Add the carrot mixture to the flour mixture and mix using a spatula; add remaining ingredients and mix well.

8. Apply non-stick spray to the pressure cooker.

9. Pour the batter evenly into the pressure cooker over the orange slices; secure lid.

10. Set pressure cooker to RICE and timer to 30 minutes.

11. When cooking is complete, remove the lid and let the cake rest for 20 minutes inside the pressure cooker.

12. Invert the cake onto a cake stand and serve.

white chocolate cheesecake

makes 8 servings

INGREDIENTS

8 vanilla cream cookies
¼ cup almonds, slivered
1 tablespoon unsalted butter
¼ cup heavy cream
8 ounces white chocolate, finely chopped
12 ounces cream cheese

¼ cup sugar
2 large eggs
1 teaspoon lemon juice
1 teaspoon vanilla extract
1 cup water

1. Preheat oven to 350 degrees; place cookies, almonds and butter into a food processor fitted with the metal S blade then secure the lid.

2. Pulse for 1 minute or until an even crumb is achieved.

3. Place a sheet of parchment paper over the base of a 7-inch springform pan; secure the ring around the pan then apply non-stick spray to the inside of the pan.

4. Press the cookie mixture into the bottom of the pan and bake for 10 minutes; let cool.

5. In a small saucepan over medium heat, bring the cream to a simmer then remove from heat; add the chocolate to the cream and stir until smooth.

6. In a mixer or food processor, combine the cream cheese and sugar; mix until very smooth.

7. While mixing, add the eggs (one at a time) through the feed tube then add the lemon juice, vanilla and white chocolate mixture; mix until smooth then transfer mixture to the cooled springform pan.

8. Wrap the pan tightly in aluminum foil; pour the water into the pressure cooker then place the pan into the pressure cooker and secure the lid.

9. Set pressure cooker to MEAT and timer to 40 minutes.

10. When cooking is complete and pressure is released from the pressure cooker, carefully remove the pan from the pressure cooker.

11. Let rest at room temperature for 30 minutes then refrigerate for 3 hours before serving.

key lime cheesecake

makes 6 to 8 servings

CRUST INGREDIENTS

10 vanilla crème wafers
2 tablespoons unsalted butter
¼ cup macadamia nuts

FILLING INGREDIENTS

3 packages (8 ounces each) cream cheese
1 can (14 ounces) sweetened condensed milk
3 large eggs
1 tablespoon all purpose flour
⅓ cup key lime juice
1 teaspoon lime zest
1 teaspoon butter nut extract
2 drops green food coloring (optional)

1. Preheat oven to 350 degrees; place a sheet of parchment paper over the base of a 7-inch springform pan.

2. Secure the ring around the springform pan; apply non-stick spray to the pan.

3. Place all crust ingredients into a food processor; process for 30 seconds or until fine crumbs are achieved then press the mixture firmly into the base of the pan.

4. Place the pan into the oven and bake for 10 minutes.

5. Place the cream cheese and milk into the food processor; process for 1 minute or until very smooth; while processing, add the eggs (one at a time) through the feed tube then continue to process for 30 seconds.

6. Add remaining filling ingredients then process for an additional 30 seconds.

7. Pour filling into the baked crust then wrap the entire springform pan in aluminum foil.

8. Pour 1 cup of water into the pressure cooker then place the pan into the pressure cooker; secure lid.

9. Set pressure cooker to MEAT and timer to 40 minutes.

10. When cooking is complete, remove the pan from the pressure cooker and let rest at room temperature for 30 minutes.

11. Refrigerate the covered cheesecake for 2 hours before serving.

hot fudge cake

makes 8 servings

INGREDIENTS

1 box (18¼ ounces) chocolate fudge cake mix
1 cup heavy cream
3 large eggs
½ cup unsalted butter
2 cups water

1. Apply non-stick spray to a 2-quart stainless steel bowl or baking insert.

2. Place all ingredients, except water, into a food processor; mix until smooth then transfer to the stainless bowl.

3. Pour water into the pressure cooker and place the bowl in the water; secure lid.

4. Set pressure cooker to MEAT and timer to 30 minutes.

5. When cooking is complete, invert onto a cake stand and serve.

index

swiss chard white bean stew 46
szechuan veggies 92

T

thai chicken curry 102
tomato florentine 16
turkey
    beet greens with smoked turkey wings 74
    lentils with italian turkey sausage 32
    pizza soup 28
    stuffed turkey breast 114
    turkey pot roast 116
    turkey ropa vieja 118

V

vegetable curry 94
vegetable stock 39
vegetables
    artichokes in lemon dill 71
    beet greens w/ turkey wings 74
    braised purple cabbage 79
    brussels sprouts w/ pearl onions 80
    buttery corn on the cob 76
    creamy spinach mashed potatoes 84
    hummus 87
    lemon dill green beans 78
    mashed potatoes with rutabaga 86
    parsnip purée with shallots 88
    spaghetti squash 77
    stuffed onions 82
    sweet beets & carrots 72
    szechuan veggies 92
    vegetable curry 94

W

wheat berry salad 54
white chocolate cheesecake 166
wild rice with dried cranberries 56
wolf's warm potato salad 90

For more of Deb's delicious ideas, please visit:
www.cookingwithdeb.com